SAGE BURNING

SAGE BURNING

Sacred Energy Cleansing Rituals

Kiera Fogg

NEW BURLINGTON

A QUARTO BOOK

First published in 2019
by New Burlington Press
The Old Brewery
6 Blundell Street
London N7 9BH

ISBN: 978-0-85762-913-5

10 9 8 7 6 5 4 3 2 1

Digital edition published in 2019

Conceived, edited, and designed by
Quarto Publishing plc
an imprint of The Quarto Group
6 Blundell Street
London N7 9BH

www.quartoknows.com
QUAR.307462

Senior editor: Kate Burkett
Senior designer: Martina Calvio
Designer: Jackie Palmer
Photographers: Dave Burton,
Jess Esposito, Erin Leslie, Phil Wilkins,
Sydney St. Mars, and Little Box of Rocks
Art director: Jess Hibbert
Publisher: Samantha Warrington

MIX
Paper from
responsible sources
FSC® C016973

CONTENTS

Meet Kiera   6
The Power of Smoke
  Cleansing   8
About this Book   10

CHAPTER 1:
Building Your Sacred Kit   12

Sacred Kit Basics   14
Sacred Sticks   16
Sacred Bowls   18
Sacred Spray   20
Incense   22
Sacred Cleansing
  with Crystals   24

CHAPTER 2:
Sacred Plants   26

Apple   28
Camomile   29
Lotus   30
Basil   31
Clover   32
Lemon   33
Rosemary   34
Cinnamon   35
Lavender   36
Dill   37

Eucalyptus   38
Ginger   39
Hibiscus   40
Peppermint   41
Palo Santo   42
Rose   43
Sage   44
Sweetgrass   45
Vanilla   46
Yarrow   47

CHAPTER 3:
Creating Your Sacred Herb
  Blend and Ritual   48

Blending   50
Drying and Wrapping   52
Burning   54
Preparing Your Space   56
Protecting Your Energy   58
Your Sacred Prayer   60
Your Custom Ritual   62

CHAPTER 4:
Sacred Herb Rituals   64

Good Luck   66
Romance   68
Rise & Shine   70

Sweet Dreams   72
Self-Expression   74
All Purpose   76
Home, Sweet Home   78
Confidence   80
Psychic Wisdom   82
Rejuvenation   84
Good Vibes   86
Self Love   88
Female Empowerment   90
Cord Cutting   92
Calling All Angels   94
Divine Health   96
Sweet Success   98
Protection   100
Newborn Wish   102
New Journeys   104
Anxiety   106
Birthday Wishes   108
Forgiveness   110
Friendship   112
Aura Cleansing   114
Crossing Over   116
Creativity   118
Overcoming Addictions   120
After an Argument   122
Blessed Marriage   124

Index   126
Credits and Bibliography   128

MEET KEIRA

Ever since I was a little girl, I've held a deep fascination with the power of nature to heal and inspire. Spending many of my childhood summers exploring the wilderness of Northern Ontario, Canada, where my family originated, I developed a firm belief that I could always turn to the healing power of nature in times of need to reconnect with my higher power.

Perhaps this is one reason why, as an adult, I chose a career in the wellness industry that resulted in launching a retail brand, called Little Box of Rocks, selling healing crystal gift sets, herb bundles and other wellness tools. Some are surprised to know that although my products and advice have been featured in a variety of large-scale media outlets like *Vogue*, *Huffington Post*, *People* and *Oprah Magazine*, I don't consider myself to be a spiritual guru by any stretch. Rather, I'm an average person – an entrepreneur and a busy mum of three – who has made it a mission to debunk the myth that meaningful spiritual practices and rituals should be reserved for the 'experts' of the world.

I certainly was no expert when I first stumbled upon the practice of energy cleansing. Ironically, my first experience with this healing modality occurred after

I received my first rejection letter from a prominent book publisher. It had been my lifelong dream to publish a book, and when I read the letter, I was crushed. In tears, I called a good friend of mine who immediately came to sweep my home with a bundle of white sage. I felt better after the visit and became captivated by this seemingly complex ritual. I soon came to learn, however, that this powerful practice is an incredibly simple tool that we can all use – and it is particularly amusing to have the opportunity to relay this anecdote in my second published book!

I firmly believe that we each hold within us all the divine wisdom and power that we will ever need to live the life of our dreams. It is my great honour to help guide you on your path to becoming your own 'expert' in this wonderful healing practice.

THE POWER OF SMOKE CLEANSING

The fragrant smoke of dried plants has been used in religious and medicinal ceremonies around the globe for thousands of years. In ancient Greece, herbs and resins were burned by priests to heal the sick, while Buddhist monks used the smoke from incense to guide their meditation. In European peasant cultures, the practice had more practical applications, as it was intended to clear parasites and bugs from domestic animals, and burned in hospitals in an effort to prevent contagion.

The use of smoke as a form of spiritual cleansing is perhaps best known as a result of the indigenous ritual of purifying, a sacred practice whereby the smoke from sweetgrass, tobacco, cedar or white sage is used in ceremonies to rid a subject of negative thoughts, energies and spirits. While the specific tools and plants used in this process can vary a great deal from tribe to tribe, all view this ancient practice as a way to shift between the physical and the spiritual realms.

Modern spiritual practices draw inspiration from these global traditions, with incense bundles becoming increasingly popular in wellness shops and even large retail shops. It isn't uncommon now for people to burn a sacred herb stick to cleanse a new home, or simply as a way to promote spiritual connection. As the practice of energy cleansing becomes better understood, more and more people are seeing the benefit of incorporating this healing modality into their everyday lives.

Case Study 1: The Golden Touch

Kim from Illinois wrote in to our shop recently. She explained that she had been having problems selling her house. After several months on the market, she followed an estate agent's advice and made a large renovation. When her house still didn't sell, she reluctantly decided to drop the price, meaning that she would lose what she had invested in the renovation. Over the next few months, the home received a handful of offers, which unfortunately all fell through.

Finally, at the suggestion of a friend, she purchased a bundle of white sage from our shop. She knew that she needed to shift her perception of the home to one of abundance, instead of her current perception of anxiety and lack. And so when she received the kit, she decided she needed to give it 'the golden touch'. She moved through the house fanning the smoke from the white sage in all directions. Each time she stepped into a room, she envisioned that the walls were turning to solid gold.

When she was finished, she asked her higher power to lead the perfect homeowners to the home.

One week later, she received not one but two offers from two different couples who had fallen in love with the house. She sold her home for 20k above the asking price, which was the same price it had initially been listed for. She couldn't believe it when she found out that the new occupants owned a prominent jewellery shop.

Case Study 2: Stupid Cupid

Having experienced one bad fling after another, my friend Myra would frequently bring me to tears of laughter with stories of her terrible experiences with men. One day, as she was regaling me with yet another dating flop, I suggested that while they made for entertaining anecdotes, she really needed to stop telling her bad dating stories. I explained that her subconscious mind would attract whatever it was most consistently told. Instead, I suggested that she describe what she wanted in an ideal partner. For good measure, I visited Myra a

few nights later with a bundle of white sage wrapped in rose and hibiscus. I instructed her to close her eyes and visualise the man of her dreams. When the ritual was complete, she agreed to hold this picture in her mind every night before bed.

'Well, your cleanse certainly must have done something,' she told me a few days later. 'Everything is going wrong!' She explained that she had dropped her phone in the bath and it had stopped working. The very next morning her car had broken down, leaving her stranded with no phone on the side of

the road. On and on she went about a myriad of other misfortunes before I finally stopped her. Clearly this was a habit that needed to be broken in other aspects of her life, too. I advised her to stay faithful, trusting that her desired outcome was in the works.

Two weeks later, Myra was picking up her car from the garage for the second time. As fortune would have it, she bumped into Jay, an old secondary school friend who wasted no time in asking her for coffee. Coffee turned into dinner and several more dates. Today they are engaged.

ABOUT THIS BOOK

Explore the ancient healing art of energy cleansing.
In this book, Kiera Fogg creates 30 custom blends that
are accompanied by healing rituals for a variety of life's
ailments, milestones and occasions.

1 Explore the basic tools and materials
that you will use to create and
conduct your rituals.

The positive traits of each plant are called out

A brief description of the plant and its healing power is provided

Accompaniments tell you what the plants can be paired with, so you can easily create your own blend

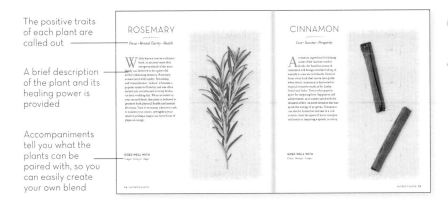

Discover the 20 most powerful plants that are commonly used for the purpose of cleansing.

Learn how to tailor your herb blend and ritual to address your own unique needs and desires.

The header outlines the purpose of each ritual

An affirmation provides you with words of inspiration

The blend's benefits are identified

Simple ingredient lists present the herbs, oils and tools needed

Step by steps set out how to conduct the ritual

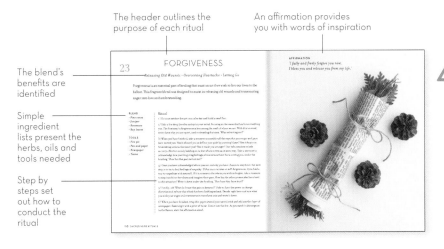

Heal, bless and protect various aspects of your life with these 30 custom-created, powerful cleansing rituals.

CHAPTER

BUILDING
YOUR
SACRED KIT

———————— • ————————

Before we delve into the exciting world of energy-cleansing rituals, we need to begin by collecting the right supplies. In this chapter, we will explore the basic tools and materials that you will use to create and conduct your rituals. We will also discuss when and how to use some of the most popular cleansing varieties.

SACRED KIT BASICS

In order to create and conduct your cleansing rituals, you will need a handful of materials to assist you. While your tool kit might grow to be quite vast and can truly include anything that inspires you, the following is a list of some basic items to get you started.

Abalone Shell

Used in traditional indigenous cleansing rituals to represent the element of water, a 12–15-cm (5–6-inch) abalone shell provides a useful container for burning loose blends or a convenient resting place for your lit sacred herb sticks.

Charcoal & Burner

Turn any dried herb or plant into loose incense with a charcoal and metal charcoal burner. While some plants can extinguish too quickly, the intense heat from the charcoal will enable most ingredients to remain lit for an extended period.

Twine

Twine is available in a wide variety of colours and thicknesses. When selecting your twine, be sure to choose one that is 100 percent cotton, which is biodegradable and safe when burned.

Feather Wand

A symbol of the element of air, use a large, ethically harvested feather wand to fan the smoke from your sacred blends over your subject and space. While you might choose to purchase a standard turkey feather wand online or at your local spiritual supply shop, you can easily make your own wand using a fallen feather of any kind.

Spray Bottle

Available at any local craft supply shop, use a 28- or 60-ml (1- or 2-oz) spray bottle to create custom mists, using filtered spring water, witch hazel and your favourite blend of essential oils.

Plants

Acting at the heart of your cleansing rituals are your carefully selected plants. Use dried flowers, herbs, oils and powders to create custom aromatic blends to suit your unique needs.

Pestle & Mortar

An especially useful tool for creating loose incense bowls, mists and homemade incense, a stone pestle and mortar will allow you to grind your plants into a fine powder.

Matches

Representing the element of fire, ignite your blends with a box of long-burn matches, which are biodegradable and therefore easily discarded as your blend disintegrates into ash.

SACRED STICKS

Creating sacred herb sticks is a wonderful way to preserve your blends, not only making for stunning visual presentation, but also allowing them to last for several uses.

WHEN TO USE

Turn to this method in more formal rituals and ceremonies, or offer a carefully wrapped sacred herb stick as a meaningful gift.

TOOLS
- *Twine*
- *Dried plants*
- *Feather wand*
- *Matches*
- *Abalone shell or heat-safe dish*
- *Water or sand*

A sacred stick is a tightly bound bundle of plants that is dried and then burned alongside a meditation or ritual. If you've ever stepped into a new-age shop or googled the words 'energy cleansing', chances are you've seen images of the traditional type of white sage stick made popular by indigenous cultures. But sacred sticks appear in a variety of other forms as well. While most sacred sticks contain a central ingredient that makes up the bulk of the blend – such as white sage, palo santo, sweetgrass or juniper – other ingredients can be incorporated just as readily, to add visual appeal and enhance the meaning.

When you are making your own, feel free to get as creative as you like. Keep it simple with a single ingredient, or embellish your sacred stick with other items like flowers, crystals and colourful twine. While it isn't necessary to wrap your blends in the form of a sacred stick, it does provide the practical advantage of making your blends last for several uses. When you have finished with your ritual, simply extinguish the tip of your stick in a bowl of sand or a small amount of water and set it aside for future use.

SACRED BOWLS

Creating a sacred bowl is a convenient and effective way of burning your blends, without the added task of tying and wrapping.

WHEN TO USE

Turn to this method for rituals that you perform on a routine basis, or in rituals that you wish to perform quickly.

TOOLS

· *Abalone shell or charcoal burner*
· *Plants*
· *Feather wand*
· *Sand*

A sacred bowl is just a dish that is used to burn your herbs in a loose-leaf format. You can turn any one of your favourite sacred sticks into an aromatic sacred bowl simply by placing its ingredients in a heat-safe dish. Many of the most common energy cleansing ingredients, such as white sage, sweetgrass and palo santo, will burn beautifully when added to a dish or abalone shell. Sacred bowls allow us to preserve our ingredients by burning small amounts at a time, making it easy to test and modify different combinations of ingredients.

Should you find that your plants do not remain lit, they can also be burned with the use of a charcoal. Simply fill a heat-resistant, metal bowl with at least 5 cm (2 inches) of sand and light a charcoal at the centre. Once your charcoal has caught, sprinkle a small amount of herbs at the centre; the extreme heat will keep them lit until they turn to ashes. Burning your blends in a sacred bowl is perhaps the quickest and easiest way of energy cleansing. When you have finished, douse the ingredients with water and discard the ashes.

SACRED SPRAY

A sacred spray is a smokeless alternative to burning your blend, which takes inspiration from the healing properties of aromatherapy.

WHEN TO USE

Turn to this method any time you wish to cleanse without the smoky smell. Take your spray with you on the go, or give your pillow a quick spritz before you go to bed.

TOOLS

· *Essential oils*
· *Spray bottle*
· *Filtered spring water*
· *Witch hazel*

Drawing on the benefits of aromatherapy, a sacred spray created with your favourite combination of essential oils is the perfect way to take your cleansing practice with you on the go. Simply add a few drops of essential oils to a small spray bottle along with witch hazel and filtered spring water to create a lovely aromatic spray to cleanse and elevate your mood.

As a general rule, a 60-ml (2-oz) spray bottle will take 20–30 drops of essential oils and 2 tablespoons of witch hazel. The remainder of the container should be filled with water. Typically a blend of two to four different types of oils works best, with one or two of these oils having a more dominant concentration. One of the great joys of creating custom mists is taking your time to experiment. You will find that blending fragrances is a deeply personal experience. While there are endless recipes to be found online and throughout this book, only you will be able to determine that perfect blend to suit your unique needs and intentions. Take your time to test out different oil combinations, tuning in to how each one makes you feel.

INCENSE

Whether it's as sticks, cones, resins or loose powders, burning incense is another easy way to cleanse your space of stagnant energy.

Incense is a clean and simple alternative to burning your herbs whole. Not only is incense available in a wide variety of formats and easily purchased at almost any wellness shop, it is also self-contained and makes very little mess. This makes it great for burning on an ongoing basis to clear out stagnant energy, or as an addition to your meditation practice.

One of the biggest issues with incense is its quality. It's important to note that incense that contains strong perfumes and filler ingredients can cause headaches and therefore do more harm than good. This is why it's best to buy from a reputable supplier who can tell you about what's in their products, ensuring that the incense is made with whole, plant-based ingredients.

Another sure-fire way to ensure the quality of your incense is to make it yourself. Incense cones are surprisingly easy to make. Simply grind your dried herbs into a loose powder using a pestle and mortar. Mix in some makko powder, an ingredient that is added to help your blend stay lit when burning, and a small amount of water using a dropper. When your blend has turned into a very light paste, use an icing cone to shape your incense and carefully dislodge it with a thin item such as a twist tie. Allow your cones to dry for 24 hours, turning once to ensure that they are fully dried. When they are ready, simply light your blend; when the flame catches, blow it out gently. Your cones can be burned in a small, heat-safe dish of sand.

WHEN TO USE
Turn to this method when
you wish to cleanse on
an ongoing basis, or
for relaxation during
meditation.

TOOLS
·*Pestle and mortar*
·*Dried plants*
·*Makko powder*
·*Sand*
·*Heat-safe dish*
·*Icing cone*
·*Water*
·*Twist tie*

SACRED CLEANSING WITH CRYSTALS

Crystals can be a powerful addition to your cleansing tool kit, as they have the unique ability to hold your positive desires and intentions long after your ritual has taken place. The following is a simple, step-by-step guide to incorporating healing crystals into your practice.

1 | Select a crystal that matches the intention of the ritual. Go into any crystal shop and you will find countless options of crystals in varying colours, shapes and sizes. When selecting your crystals, be sure to choose a crystal that holds the energy you wish to attract. For instance, if you are conducting a ritual for romance, you might choose to work with Rose Quartz, the stone of unconditional love. If you are intending to attract success, you might choose Citrine or Pyrite, stones for stamina and prosperity.

2 | Find a way to incorporate your crystal in or near your blend. Not only will this allow the energy of the crystal to enhance the blend, it also creates a stunning visual component. If you are working with a sacred stick, bind a crystal to the base using thin rope or twine. For loose blends, set a crystal in your abalone shell. (Please note: the crystal can get very hot.) For mists and oils, simply drop it into the bottle to infuse your blend with the energy of the crystal.

3 | Include your crystal in meditation as part of your ritual. Simply hold your crystal in the palm of your hands, or place it on a comfortable spot on your body, such as your chest or forehead. Close your eyes and allow yourself to tune in to the energy of the crystal.

4 | Keep your crystal close by during and after your ritual. Either set it in a high-traffic room, where you will see it often, or tuck it in your purse or pocket, or under your pillow. Doing so will serve as a reminder of the positive intentions you've set through your ritual.

Types of Crystals

ROSE QUARTZ

Widely known as the stone of unconditional love, this soft pink stone is especially useful in rituals for friendship and romance. Place it in a high-traffic room when you have finished with it to promote a peaceful and harmonious environment, or tuck it under your pillow to attract love of all kinds.

AMETHYST

A wonderful 'good-for-anything' gem, this purple beauty will go to work in whatever way it is needed, but is especially useful in rituals for mental, physical and spiritual health. Allow it to promote deep spiritual wisdom.

CLEAR QUARTZ

An extremely versatile cleanser and amplifier of energy, Clear Quartz has the unique ability to take on any wish or intention. Program this gem to help you accomplish your desired outcomes.

PYRITE

Offering the energy of fire, Pyrite is believed to infuse your workspace with positive energy. Turn to this golden beauty to enhance rituals for success, confidence and positive energy.

CITRINE

Known to hold the energy of the sun, Citrine is a powerful cleanser and rejuvenator. Include it in rituals for health, wealth and prosperity. When placed in the furthest left corner of the home (relative to the front door), this yellow stone is believed to attract prosperity.

SELENITE

One of the most frequently used crystals for space clearing. Turn to this powdery white gem for physical protection and to inspire a connection to angelic realms.

KYANITE

This powdery blue blade is believed to instantly align the body's chakras. Include it in rituals where the intention is realignment, detoxification or rejuvenation. Meditate with this stone to promote a sense of inner peace and harmony.

CHAPTER

SACRED
PLANTS

———— • ————

As you continue to delve into the world of energy cleansing, you'll find that there are literally thousands of different plants to choose from when creating your blends. In this chapter, we take a closer look at some of the most useful and versatile plants, based on both their pleasant fragrances and powerful metaphysical properties.

APPLE

Love · Beauty · Wisdom

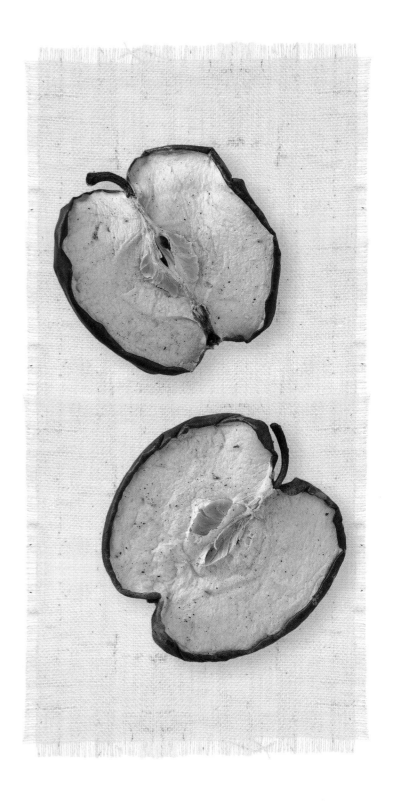

Simple and readily available at any market or supermarket, the apple is one of the most common fruits eaten in North America and Europe. This doesn't mean, however, that it doesn't carry a significant weight metaphorically and metaphysically. This sweet fruit has been a part of various folk tales for thousands of years, holding associations with love, beauty, fidelity, marriage and the afterlife. To prepare an apple for cleansing, simply set it in the sun to dry.

GOES WELL WITH

Cinnamon, Palo Santo, Vanilla

CAMOMILE

Peace · Purification · Protection

Best known for its calming effects for use in teas, lotions and medicines, camomile was so revered by the ancient Egyptians that it was dedicated to the Gods. This daisy-like flower is associated with the element of water, making it particularly useful for cleansing and purification purposes. Include camomile in rituals for easing stress and assisting with sleep, as it is known to inspire peace and tranquility. Its apple-like scent is cheerful and fresh, making it an effective aid for easing depression and anxiety.

GOES WELL WITH

Lavender, Rose, Lemon

LOTUS

Rebirth · Fortitude · Divinity

Considered one of the most sacred flowers in spirituality today, the lotus was a prominent emblem in ancient Eastern cultures. To understand the symbolism of this revered flower, one must look at its remarkable life cycle. With roots based in muddy waters, the lotus sinks beneath the murky river every night and then miraculously emerges the next morning with its petals pristine and clear of residue. It is an emblem of strength, divinity and resurrection. Add the dried petals of this flower to rituals when you wish to inspire courage, wisdom and unwavering strength.

GOES WELL WITH

Bergamot, Clove, Jasmine

BASIL

Health · Happiness · Protection

Widely known as a culinary herb and a member of the mint family, basil is an easily accessed cleansing ingredient that is incredibly versatile. Exuding a very positive and uplifting energy, this leafy plant offers a rich and spicy aroma that is known to awaken the senses and promote a joyful state of mind. A wonderful 'good-for-anything' herb, in ancient Greek lore basil was believed to guard the wellbeing of the family when kept in the home. Include dried basil leaves in rituals for prosperity, health, love, protection and wellbeing of any kind.

GOES WELL WITH

Grapefruit, Bergamot, Cedarwood

CLOVER

Faith · Hope · Prosperity

Most famous for the lucky four-leafed clover, the heart-shaped leaves of this plant typically grow in clusters of three. Turn to the clover when you wish to attract luck, success and good fortune of any kind. Further, its connection with the element of air makes it effective in balancing the mind and heart. Include it in rituals for healing emotional wounds and re-establishing a sense of balance. Its fragrance is light and unimposing, similar to that of freshly cut grass, making it an easy addition to a wide variety of blends.

GOES WELL WITH

Peppermint, Vanilla, Lavender

LEMON

Purification · Protection · Energy Boost

Refreshing and rejuvenating, lemon is a powerful cleanser and detoxifier. Turn to this zesty fruit to eliminate unwanted energy and assist in inspiring complete spiritual and physical harmony. Add dried lemon peel or lemon essential oil to your blend when you wish to release stress, enhance your mood or inspire an energetic pick-me-up. Lemon is also known to be a powerful guard against lower energies, making it a natural addition to rituals for protection.

GOES WELL WITH

Peppermint, Rosemary, Pine

ROSEMARY

Focus · Mental Clarity · Health

Widely known now as a culinary herb, in ancient times this evergreen shrub of the mint family was believed to be a powerful aid for enhancing memory. Rosemary is associated with loyalty, friendship and remembrance. Indeed, it became a popular symbol of fidelity and was often tucked into wreaths and worn by brides on their wedding day. When included in your sacred blend, this plant is believed to promote both physical health and mental alertness. Turn to rosemary when you wish to awaken your senses, strengthen your mind or perhaps inspire an extra boost of physical energy.

GOES WELL WITH

Ginger, Juniper, Sage

CINNAMON

Love · Success · Prosperity

A common ingredient for baking some of the tastiest comfort foods, the familiar aroma of cinnamon will bring a similar feeling of warmth to your sacred blends. Derived from a tree bark that curves into quills when dried, cinnamon is harvested in tropical countries such as Sri Lanka, Brazil and India. Turn to this popular spice for inspiring love, happiness and achievement, as it is associated with the element of fire, an earth element that can spark the energy of progress. Cinnamon can also be burned as incense in a sick room to clear the space of lower energies and assist in inspiring a speedy recovery.

GOES WELL WITH

Clove, Orange, Ginger

LAVENDER

Love • Relaxation • Serenity

A wonderful addition to almost any sacred stick, this lovely purple flower is useful for a wide variety of healing purposes. It is perhaps best known for its calming effects, so include this powerful plant in any sleep or relaxation ritual. Lavender can also be used to attract love, luck and good health. You may also choose to decorate your sacred stick with dried lavender buds to promote a sense of protection, wellbeing and joy.

GOES WELL WITH

Vanilla, Orange, Jasmine

DILL

Luck · Romance · Prosperity

Typically used for the purposes of flavouring food, this aromatic herb, which is a member of the parsley family, should not be overlooked when it comes to energy cleansing. Holding a masculine energy associated with the element of fire, dill is particularly useful in attracting romantic love. In fact, it is believed that bathing with this green, feathered plant can make one irresistible to the opposite sex. Include dried dill leaves or seeds in your sacred blends to boost romance, or to attract prosperity and good fortune of all kinds.

GOES WELL WITH

Star Anise, Fennel, Apple

EUCALYPTUS

Health · Purification · Protection

There are more than 700 species of this evergreen plant, which are found predominantly in Australia. If you look closely at the sickle-shaped leaves of the eucalyptus, you will see tiny oil glands covering the surface. The potent oil finds many uses in fragrances, flu medications, insecticides and even fuels. Similar to white sage, eucalyptus is known for its powerful cleansing and protective qualities. Use it to make a sacred stick or gather a few dried leaves and burn them as incense.

GOES WELL WITH

Lemongrass, Peppermint, Cedarwood

GINGER

Passion · Progress · Prosperity

Once considered sacred by the ancient Greeks and Romans, ginger has been a well-known medicinal aid for thousands of years. In fact, ginger was thought to be so powerful that in medieval times it was believed to have originated from the Garden of Eden. The greyish-yellow root of this plant will add a pungent and spicy aroma to your sacred blend, along with a powerful energetic kick. It holds the energy of fire, so include ginger in your blend when you wish to add a serious boost of energy to your ritual. It is especially useful in blends for passion, success and progress.

GOES WELL WITH

Bergamot, Frankincense, Lemon

HIBISCUS

Passion · Femininity · Creativity

A treasured evergreen shrub whose blossoms last just a day or two, the hibiscus flower carries a strong association with the divine feminine. Known to clear and re-energize the first and second chakras — our centres for reproduction, creativity and emotional freedom — hibiscus is useful in bolstering physical energy, balancing hormones and igniting passion. Add this trumpet-shaped beauty to your sacred blend when addressing issues related to love, creativity, reproduction and sexuality.

GOES WELL WITH

Rose, Vanilla, Lavender

PEPPERMINT

Prosperity · Growth · Renewal

A hybrid species of spearmint and water mint, peppermint is a convenient and accessible plant for the home gardener. Grow this versatile herb in a moist container, away from direct sunlight. The leaves of the peppermint plant can be collected as soon as the flowers begin to open, and may be dried for use in food or tea. Renowned for its cooling menthol sensation, peppermint is often used in aromatherapy to ease stress and clear the mind. Include it in your sacred blend to promote happiness, luck, success and renewal.

GOES WELL WITH
Juniper, Orange, Lavender

PALO SANTO

Stress Release • Protection •
Good Fortune

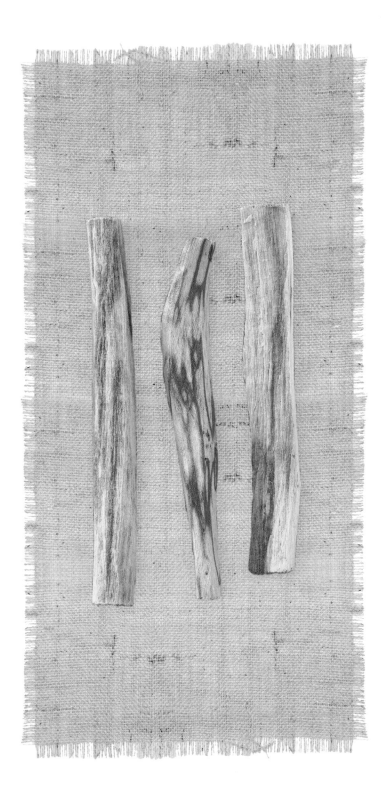

Harvested from the naturally fallen branches of the palo santo tree on the coast of South America, this aromatic wood carries notes of pine, mint and lemon. When burned, palo santo will bring an inviting fragrance that is known to ease anxiety, elevate moods and help to prepare the mind for meditation. To burn it, simply light the end of a stick and carefully point it downwards until the fire catches. Blow out the flame and allow the comforting aroma to fill the air.

GOES WELL WITH

Rose, Peppermint, Lemongrass

ROSE

Love · Happiness · Friendship

Most commonly associated with love and beauty, it's no wonder that the rose is considered the queen of all flowers. Useful for a wide variety of purposes, the meaning of this sweet-scented flower varies depending on its colour. Traditionally, red roses symbolise love, pink roses symbolise joy and gratitude, orange roses symbolise passion and white roses symbolise purity. Add dried roses or rose petals to any sacred stick to instantly enhance its beauty and infuse your blend with the joyful energy of this majestic plant.

GOES WELL WITH

Hibiscus, Jasmine, Patchouli

SAGE

Purification · Protection · Wisdom

One of the most renowned plants for energy clearing, sage is king in the world of cleansing. In indigenous cultures it has been used for thousands of years in sacred purifying rituals. When burned, it produces a thick, grey smoke that will quickly fill a space with a potent, earthy fragrance. Associated with the element of air, sage is known to purify a space of negative energy and help us to release that which is no longer serving us. It is also known to offer protection, spiritual healing and wisdom.

GOES WELL WITH

Lemon, Ylang Ylang, Rose

SWEETGRASS

Peace • Purification • Positive Energy

N amed for its sweet, aromatic fragrance, sweetgrass is believed to attract good spirits and positive energy. One of the most common plants used for cleansing, this herb typically comes braided and is considered sacred among indigenous cultures. When added to your blend, it will both cleanse your subject of lower frequencies while restoring it with positive energy. The aroma of sweetgrass is gentle and unobtrusive, making it a welcome addition to rituals that are performed on a regular basis.

GOES WELL WITH

Lavender, Cedarwood, Sandalwood

VANILLA

Love • Peace • Good Fortune

A standard ingredient in scented candles, beauty products and baked goods, the sweet and comforting fragrance of vanilla is easily paired with almost any scent. Include vanilla pods in your wand, or crush the beans in a mortar bowl and burn them as incense to create a warm and welcoming atmosphere that inspires peace, love and good fortune. A powerful mood enhancer, vanilla is known to ease stress and calm the mind, making it a particularly useful ingredient in relaxation and sleep rituals.

GOES WELL WITH

Jasmine, Orange, Cinnamon

YARROW

Courage · Wisdom · Protection

O ffering strength, courage and protection, yarrow's botanical name, *Achillea*, is a direct reference to the Greek hero Achilles, who used this revered plant to treat the wounds of his soldiers during the Trojan War. Growing in small clusters of white, yellow or pink flowers, yarrow is a plant of the daisy family that makes the perfect complement to sacred blends for heightening spiritual wisdom, enhancing mental clarity and shielding us from negative energy.

GOES WELL WITH

Ylang Ylang, Camomile, Lavender

CHAPTER

3

CREATING YOUR SACRED HERB BLEND AND RITUAL

———•———

Now that we've explored the various components of an effective cleansing kit, it's time to get to work. You might be surprised to know that a successful sacred herb blend and ritual is incredibly simple to create and conduct. In this chapter, you will become an expert in tailoring them to address your own unique needs and desires.

BLENDING

With so many options to choose from, creating a sacred blend that is both meaningful and aromatic can feel somewhat overwhelming. Becoming familiar with the following plant families can help to narrow down the options when selecting your cleansing ingredients. As a general rule, plants within the same family tend to blend well together, or with a handful of other compatible families. It's important to remember, however, that blending is a very personal experience with no hard-and-fast rules. Trust your senses and if you find yourself drawn to a specific plant, go with it!

Florals

Most often used in beauty and skincare products, plants in the floral family carry a sweet and heady aroma, which can range from mild to sharp. Include this family in your blend when you wish to elevate your mood, balance hormones or inspire romance. Florals tend to blend well with trees, citruses and spices. Examples include lavender, rose, vanilla, geranium and jasmine.

Citrus

Frequently used in cleaning products for antibacterial purposes, plants in the citrus family offer a fresh and sweet fragrance that can serve as an energetic pick-me-up. Include citrus plants in your blends when you wish to rejuvenate and detoxify. Plants from the citrus family tend to blend well with florals, spices and trees. Examples include grapefruit, lemon, orange and bergamot.

Trees

Plants within the tree family are often seen in cold and flu medications to alleviate upper respiratory symptoms. These plants typically offer a fresh cooling sensation that can help with muscle tension. Turn to the tree family when you wish to ease stress and anxiety, boost physical health or assist with sleep. Tree family plants are the most versatile, typically blending well with any plant family. Examples include eucalyptus, tea tree, cedarwood and all evergreens.

Herbs

Most often used as culinary ingredients, plants within the herb family tend to act as powerful mental stimulants. Turn to herbal plants to assist with focus, memory retention and low physical energy. This family tends to blend well with the tree family. Examples include rosemary, basil, peppermint, spearmint and sage.

Resins

Plants within the resin family typically offer an earthy and musky fragrance known to have a powerful grounding effect. Particularly useful for easing stress, anxiety and depression, many resins are also traditionally seen as aphrodisiacs. Resins tend to blend well with citrus, trees and florals. Examples include frankincense, sandalwood, patchouli and myrrh.

Spices

Typically used in our favourite baking and cooking recipes, plants within the spice family offer a familiar, warm 'kick' that is capable of tickling the back of our throats. Often thought of as powerful stimulants, turn to the spice family to infuse your sacred blend with the energy of power, strength and success. Spices tend to mix well with florals and citruses. Examples include ginger, cinnamon, nutmeg and clove.

DRYING & WRAPPING

While pre-wrapped sacred sticks are becoming more readily available in modern wellness shops, it can be much more fun and meaningful to do it ourselves. The following is a step-by-step guide to drying and wrapping your own gorgeous sacred sticks.

Drying

Plants for your sacred blends can be dried either before you wrap your stick or after. Here are the steps for drying your ingredients before you wrap your stick.

1 | Begin by gathering your plants into a small bundle. If you are harvesting the plants yourself, be sure to cut them close to the ground to ensure a long enough stem for tying.

2 | Using a thin piece of string or twine, tie a tight knot at the base of your bundle. Leave an extra 15–30 cm (6–12 inches) to be used for hanging.

3 | Hang your plants upside down in a dry, well-ventilated area away from direct sunlight. A spare bedroom or cupboard works well. Drying time will typically range between two and three weeks. Dried plants will remain fragrant for six to twelve months.

Wrapping

Sacred sticks can be wrapped in a lot of different ways — criss-cross, spiral or simply bound at the base. The criss-cross is my personal favourite, as it adds a beautiful finishing touch to any blend. Here are the steps for wrapping the perfect criss-crossed sacred stick.

1 | Gather your ingredients into a tight bundle and hold it securely at the base. Double the length of your twine and begin by wrapping it around the base several times.

2 | When it feels secure, move up the stick in a criss-cross pattern. If your plants have not been dried before wrapping, be sure to bind them with extra tightness, as the plants will shrink after they have dried.

3 | When you reach the top, move down the length of the stick once again, making sure you follow the lines you've already wrapped. Secure with a knot at the base of your stick.

BURNING

Now that you've done all the prep work, it's time to ignite your blend and enjoy its therapeutic benefits. As you do this, however, it is important to take proper safety precautions to ensure that your plants burn safely and effectively.

Loose Plants

When burning loose herbs and plants as incense, it's important to note that they will burn best with the use of a charcoal. To begin, place the charcoal disk in a charcoal-suitable burner. Always make sure you use a fireproof and shatterproof dish. Containers made from seashell, wood or glass are not appropriate, as they are likely to crack with the extreme heat. Light the disk on one edge and watch the flame travel across. After a minute or so, you may add your loose herbs to the cupped area as desired.

Wrapped Plants

Wrapped sacred blends are wonderfully simple to burn. Simply ignite the end of the stick and allow the flame to catch for a few moments, before very gently blowing out the fire. It is important to ensure that the twine or string you are using is heat-friendly. Natural materials such as hemp or cotton are ideal. Steer clear of string that is stretchy or contains plastic.

Wooden Sticks

When igniting wooden sticks such as palo santo, birch or sandalwood, light the end of the stick and angle it downwards slightly. Allow the flame to run up the length of the wood for a couple of centimetres or so. When the flame has caught, gently blow it out.

PREPARING YOUR SPACE

Preparing your space is critical, as it sets the tone for the entire ritual. Imagine that you are clearing an energetic path, similar to a trail in the woods. You could simply plough ahead without first forging this path, but the ride would not be as pleasant. Here are four simple steps to take to ensure that your environment is ready.

1 | Set your intention
The most important step in all forms of energy work is becoming clear on your intentions. It is often said that where intention goes, energy flows. Take a moment to clarify your intentions for the ritual. What specific outcomes do you hope to manifest?

2 | Open the windows
Fresh air goes a long way, especially when it comes to cleansing. When we perform an energetic cleansing, we are asking the negative energy to exit – and so, naturally, it needs a place to go. Open the windows to make sure this energy (and the smoke) can escape.

3 | Clean your home
Consider the way you feel after your home has had a thorough cleaning. There is an atmospheric shift and it just feels so much better, doesn't it? Cleaning the home is one of the quickest ways to clear out stagnant energy – and the more meticulous you are, the better. Before beginning your ritual, invest some time in tidying up the clutter, vacuuming, dusting, wiping countertops, etc.

4 | Cleanse yourself and your tools
Finally, take a moment before you begin to fan the smoke over yourself and your tools. This is something that is easily done when you are protecting your energy.

PROTECTING YOUR ENERGY

Our energetic bodies are constantly changing with our emotions, thoughts and surroundings, so it's important to take proper measures to protect ourselves frequently, especially when performing our healing work. The following protection method can be done alongside every cleansing ritual.

1 | Close your eyes and take several deep breaths, with the intention of quieting the mind.

2 | Imagine that a golden light is surrounding you. As you breathe in and out, imagine that this light is forming an energetic shield in the shape of a large, golden sphere. As you sit inside this sphere, imagine that from the outside it takes on the appearance of a mirror, reflecting everything that is outside it.

3 | Ask your higher power to bless and guide the ritual, while shielding you from negative energy. When you feel ready, you may begin your cleansing ritual.

4 | When you have finished with your ritual, always remember to close the session by thanking your higher power and asking that you continue to be blessed and protected throughout the rest of your day.

YOUR SACRED PRAYER

A sacred prayer is a call to the Universe that is designed to accompany your ritual and reflect the specific intentions that you have set. Here are a few examples:

Invoking Miracles

'Thank you for the miracles, all in your perfect ways and all in your perfect timing.'

Receiving Divine Abundance

'Thank you for the divine health, wealth and abundance that flows to me in all ways.'

Releasing Unhealthy Attachments

'I fully and freely release that which no longer serves me. All is well.'

Self-worth

'I choose to release the opinions of others. It bears no weight on my self-worth.'

Physical Health

'I love my body and my body loves me in return.'

Self-expression

'God speaks through me.'

WRITE YOUR OWN

Your sacred prayer should be stated at least once during your ritual, and then repeated as frequently as possible throughout your day. Here are three simple steps to writing your own.

1 | Set a clear intention. What specific outcomes do you wish to manifest?

2 | Decide on two or three key words related to your intention.

3 | Write one or two sentences that succinctly reflect your desired outcome. This statement should be made with gratitude, as if it has already occurred.

YOUR CUSTOM RITUAL

It is important to keep in mind that there is no wrong way to create a ritual. You are the master here, so you cannot get it wrong. Your customised ritual may include anything from a simple walk through the home with a lit sacred stick to a personal smoke cleanse or a quiet meditation. Feel free to get as creative as you want. Here is what your ritual might look like from start to finish:

1 Set your intentions
Decide on the specific outcomes you wish to manifest.

2 Select your method
Will you be using a sacred stick, a spray, an oil, bath bomb or tea? What kind of tools will you need? Will it include a visualisation?

3 Prepare your space
Take the time to tidy up your space. Open the windows to allow the smoke and lower energy to escape.

4 Protect your energy
Connect with your higher power and ask for divine protection.

5 Conduct your cleanse
Let your creativity be your guide. Walk through your space while directing the smoke in the areas you wish to cleanse, or simply sit in quiet meditation.

6 Close the ritual
Thank your higher power and state your sacred prayer.

SACRED HERB
RITUALS

———— • ————

In this section you will find 30 custom-crafted blends and rituals to inspire some of the most common areas of life. Tweak them to suit your individual needs, only using them as a guide, or follow the steps verbatim to eliminate the guesswork and skip straight to the fun of energy cleansing.

1

GOOD LUCK

Joy · Prosperity · Good Fortune

This fresh and fragrant blend is designed to attract good fortune of all kinds, from good health, to happy relationships, to material wealth and abundance. Allow this simple ritual to offer a pick-me-up on days when your energy is low, or assist in calming the nerves before an important event or ceremony.

BLEND
- *Sweetgrass*
- *Bamboo*
- *Peppermint*
- *Purple flowers of any kind*
- *Orange peel*
- *Star anise*
- *Clover (optional)*

CRYSTAL
- *Citrine or Pyrite*

TOOLS
- *Gold twine*
- *Heat-safe dish*
- *Feather wand*

Ritual

1 | Sit quietly alone and away from distractions. Close your eyes and ask your spirit guides to bless and protect you as you conduct this ritual.

2 | Light your sacred stick in a heat-safe dish or abalone shell.

3 | Holding your Citrine or Pyrite crystal, close your eyes and take several deep breaths, imagining that you are expelling a dark fog with every exhalation. This fog represents all tension, fear and stress. Watch as it leaves your body and evaporates into the smoke.

4 | When you feel ready, envision that the crystal you are holding is emanating a beautiful golden light that begins to flood your entire being. Imagine it moving up your arms and down your legs. Breathe it into your lungs and envision it moving up through your neck and to the top of your head.

5 | The blend is wrapped in gold twine to represent your path to prosperity and good fortune. Imagine yourself walking down this golden path and visualise your goals and desires coming to fruition before you in full colour. When you arrive, you feel a sense of completion wash over you as you envision yourself living out your desires in as much detail as possible.

6 | When you have finished, open your eyes. Use your feather wand to sweep the smoke over your body, while repeating the affirmation until you feel a sense of completion. Thank your spirit guides and ask that they close this ritual.

AFFIRMATION

*'The path I walk is golden,
and I am blessed at every turn.'*

2

ROMANCE

Love · Passion · Intimacy

This blend is intended to spark a sense of deep romantic connection. Burn it to attract a new relationship or to promote a deeper sense of passion and intimacy with your current love. Perform this ritual alone or with your partner, making it unique by setting a special intention for your love life.

BLEND
- *White sage*
- *Rose*
- *Geranium or hibiscus essential oil, 2–3 drops*
- *Dill*

CRYSTAL
- *Clear Quartz (two if performing with your partner)*

TOOLS
- *Twine*
- *Music*
- *Heat-safe dish*
- *Feather wand*
- *Three pieces of paper*
- *A pen*
- *Three pink or red candles*

Ritual

1 | Set the mood with a special song.

2 | Light your sacred stick in a heat-safe dish and begin by fanning the smoke over yourself (and your partner). Close your eyes and ask your higher power to bless this ritual with unconditional love.

3 | Now, holding your Clear Quartz crystal, set three intentions that relate to your love life: one for your past, one for your present, and one for your future. For example, if you are setting an intention for your past, you might say, 'I intend to release lingering wounds from my relationship with (insert name).' When you are ready, write these three wishes down on three separate pieces of paper.

4 | Your candles are intended to act as symbols of the infinite flame of divine love that burns for your past, present and future. Light them now.

5 | Roll up the first intention (the one representing your past) and very carefully burn it in your heat-safe dish, keeping a bowl of water close for safety. Repeat this for the present and future.

6 | When you have finished, fan the smoke from your sacred stick over yourself, repeating the affirmation.

7 | Clear Quartz is believed to take on the energy of its owner. Your crystal is now charged with your three intentions. Carry it with you to attract love. If you have performed this ritual with a partner, you may choose to exchange crystals to keep his or her energy close to you.

AFFIRMATION

'I lovingly cut ties with the past and commit myself to a love-filled present and future.'

RISE & SHINE

Joy · Vitality · Purification

Start your day in the best of spirits with this powerful morning ritual, which offers a vibrant blend of aromas designed to provide an immediate pick-me-up. Add this ritual to your daily routine, or on days when your energy and focus are especially needed. After wrapping your sacred stick, set aside the extra ingredients to make a soothing morning tea.

BLEND
- *Lemons, peel for stick and juice for tea*
- *Lemongrass, plus extra for tea*
- *Rosemary, plus extra for tea*
- *Peppermint, plus extra for tea*
- *Vanilla pod, plus extra for tea*
- *Raspberries, for the tea*
- *Lavender, for the stick*

TOOLS
- *Twine*
- *Water, 500 ml (18 oz)*
- *Pot*
- *Two heat-safe dishes*
- *Feather wand*
- *Teacup*

Ritual

1 | After your sacred stick is wrapped, set your extra ingredients aside and bring water to boil in a small pot.

2 | Squeeze two lemons and place the juice in a heat-safe dish. Add lemongrass, rosemary, peppermint, a vanilla pod and the raspberries.

3 | Pour boiling water over the ingredients in the heat-safe bowl and allow it to cool enough to drink.

4 | When your tea is ready, sit in a quiet place and ask your higher power to bless this ritual.

5 | Burn your sacred stick in another heat-safe dish, looking into the smoke as it rises. Envision your day as it unfolds from start to finish. Allow your mind to drift peacefully as you envision the very best of outcomes transpiring. The goal is to put yourself in a joyful state of anticipation and gratitude for the blessings that are to unfold.

6 | When you have finished drinking your tea, extinguish your sacred stick and set it aside for another day.

7 | State your affirmation to close the ritual and thank your higher power.

AFFIRMATION

*'My cup is filled with infinite
good favour.'*

4

SWEET DREAMS

Restful Sleep · Relaxation · Guided Dreams

Transition into a peaceful sleep and guided dreams with this soothing sleep ritual, designed to calm the mind and help you release the stress of a busy day. Intended for daily use, this ritual is simple and quick, with a light and soothing mist that will have you looking forward to bedtime every day.

BLEND
- *Filtered spring water*
- *Lavender essential oil, 10 drops*
- *Vanilla essential oil, 8 drops*
- *Orange essential oil, 8 drops*
- *Jasmine essential oil, 2 drops*
- *Witch hazel, 2 tbsp*

CRYSTAL
- *Amethyst*

TOOLS
- *60 ml (2 oz) spray bottle*

Ritual

1 | Fill one-third of your spray bottle with filtered spring water. Add the remaining blend ingredients.

2 | Cleanse your Amethyst by holding it under water and asking your higher power to charge it with divine wisdom and harmony. Add it to your spray bottle and shake well.

3 | Close your eyes and think of one thing in your day for which you are grateful.

4 | Open your eyes and spray the air in front of you. Inhale deeply.

5 | Repeat steps two and three, two more times.

6 | When you have thought of three things that you are grateful for, spray your pillow, turn off the lights and crawl into bed, breathing deeply and repeating your affirmation with every exhalation until your mind drifts away.

AFFIRMATION
'I choose peace.'

5

SELF-EXPRESSION

Assertiveness • Clear Communication • Authenticity

Free your voice with this powerful ritual designed to assist in releasing energetic blockages related to the throat chakra, your centre for communication. Using the energy of Kyanite, a powdery blue gem that is known to promote effective communication, this unique blend is intended to help you to connect with your most authentic, courageous and assertive self. Turn to this ritual before an important speech, meeting or conference call.

BLEND
- *Camomile*
- *Ginger*
- *Lavender*
- *Queen of the meadow*
- *Thyme*
- *White sage*
- *Blue flowers of any kind*

CRYSTAL
- *Kyanite (or any other blue crystal)*

TOOLS
- *Twine, plus blue twine for wrapping the crystal*
- *Heat-safe dish*
- *Feather wand*

Ritual

1 | Wrap your blend tightly with twine. Use the blue twine to fasten a piece of Kyanite to the base. Blue is significant as it is the colour related to your throat chakra, your energetic centre for communication.

2 | Light your sacred stick in a heat-safe dish and gently fan the smoke over yourself, asking that your higher power assists in clearing any existing energetic blockages. Set the dish aside and close your eyes.

3 | Now, taking several deep breaths, imagine that the smoke is a rich, royal blue. Inhale this colour, allowing it to flood your body. Hold it for a moment and then exhale. As your breath leaves your body, imagine that it is the colour brown. This colour represents the energetic blockages that are now leaving your system.

4 | When you feel that you have exhaled all that which has been holding you back, open your eyes and repeat your affirmation aloud.

5 | Thank your higher power to close this ritual.

AFFIRMATION

'I express myself fully and freely, with the voice of love.'

6 ALL PURPOSE

Intention Setting · Realignment · Renewal

A simple 'all-purpose' recipe, turn to this ritual when you wish to release negative energy of any kind. Allow this potent blend to assist in releasing unwanted habits and thought patterns, while shifting your focus in a new direction going forwards.

BLEND
- *White sage*
- *Eucalyptus*
- *Baby's breath*
- *Purple flowers of any kind*
- *Basil (optional)*

CRYSTAL
- *Amethyst*

TOOLS
- *Twine*
- *Heat-safe dish*
- *Feather wand*

Ritual

1 | Ignite your blend and lie in a quiet, comfortable place. Close your eyes and ask your higher power to bless this ritual.

2 | Imagine that you are standing on a beautiful sandy beach. Out of the corner of your eye, you catch a glimpse of a glistening purple crystal. It's the most stunning piece of Amethyst you've ever seen. Amethyst is often referred to as the 'master healer', as it is known to be useful in a wide variety of circumstances. You move towards it and pick it up, immediately feeling it go to work with regards to your current situation.

3 | Looking out before you now, you set your eyes on a beautiful violet lake. You've never seen anything like it, and immediately you feel a connection to this healing body of water. As it draws you towards it, you feel compelled to enter the water.

4 | Floating blissfully in the morning sun, you begin to feel a warm tingling sensation move through your body. It starts at the top of your head and moves down your neck and spine, through your chest and stomach, and down your legs. When it reaches the very tips of your toes, you realise that the tension in your body has completely washed away, having been transmuted into this magical lake where you are now floating with more peace than ever before.

5 | You are enjoying this new sense of tranquility so much that you decide to set a new intention for your life, fully committed to its manifestation. Still holding your special piece of Amethyst, you say this intention out loud, before releasing the Amethyst into the water and allowing it to sink to the bottom.

6 | Thank your higher power to close this ritual. Repeat your affirmation several times throughout your day, keeping your Amethyst with you.

AFFIRMATION

'I release that which no longer serves me and fully commit to (fill in the blank).'

7 HOME, SWEET HOME

Space Clearing · Housewarming · New Home

Designed to renew and restore the energy of your living space, this ritual is for when you wish to clear your environment of negative frequencies. Your home is an extension of you that affects so much of how you feel on a daily basis. Intended to inspire an overall sense of wellbeing, this ritual can be practised when you move into a new home, after a guest enters or simply as a regular form of energetic cleaning. This blend also makes a lovely housewarming or hostess gift.

BLEND
- *Sweetgrass*
- *Pine*
- *White sage*
- *Yarrow*
- *Basil (optional)*

CRYSTAL
- *Citrine*
- *Rose Quartz*

TOOLS
- *Obsidian arrowhead*
- *Twine*
- *Heat-safe dish*
- *Feather wand*

Ritual

1 | Prepare your home by giving it a thorough cleaning. Vacuum, wash floors and tidy up as much as possible.

2 | Open all windows in your home to allow stagnant energy to exit.

3 | Place your healing crystals according to the following Feng Shui principles: Citrine in the furthest left-hand corner of the home, respective to the front door; Rose Quartz in a high-traffic room, such as the living room or kitchen; and the Obsidian arrowhead at the front door, underneath the doormat.

4 | Light your sacred stick in a heat-safe dish. Starting at the lowest level of the home, begin by first fanning the smoke over yourself. Ask your higher power to assist you in dispelling all negative energy within your own energetic body and your environment.

5 | Using your feather wand, slowly move through your home, repeating the affirmation and directing the smoke towards the four walls in each room.

6 | Once the smoke has dissipated, you may close the windows. Thank your higher power to mark the end of the ritual.

AFFIRMATION

'I release this space of negative energy.
Only positive energy is of influence here.'

8

CONFIDENCE

Courage · Self-Assurance · Strength

This simple blend combines three powerful essential oils to boost confidence and raise your spiritual vibrations. Turn to this ritual before an important work presentation or meeting, or any time you require courage and strength.

BLEND
- *Filtered spring water*
- *Orange essential oil, 12 drops*
- *Lavender essential oil, 7 drops*
- *Patchouli essential oil, 7 drops*
- *Witch hazel, 2 tbsp*

CRYSTAL
- *Small Carnelian*

TOOLS
- *60 ml (2 oz) spray bottle*

Ritual

1 | Fill one-third of your spray bottle with filtered spring water. Add the remaining blend ingredients.

2 | Cleanse your Carnelian by holding it under water and asking your higher power to charge it with confidence, courage and strength.

3 | Place the Carnelian in the bottle and close the lid tightly. Shake well.

4 | Mist the air in front of you and inhale deeply throughout the day as needed, while quietly repeating your affirmation.

AFFIRMATION

*'I direct my fate with wisdom, conviction
and confidence.'*

9   PSYCHIC WISDOM

Intuition · Psychic Knowledge · Clarity

This blend is designed to strengthen spiritual awareness and help to connect you with your natural psychic abilities. Turn to it any time you are in need of spiritual insights, wisdom and clarity. Practise this ritual daily, or as often as possible, to enhance your intuition.

BLEND
- *Palo santo*
- *Lavender*
- *Yarrow*
- *Baby's breath*

CRYSTAL
- *Amethyst*

TOOLS
- *Twine*
- *White candle*
- *Heat-safe dish*
- *Feather wand*

Ritual

1 | Light your candle and sit in a quiet and comfortable position. Ask your higher power to bless and protect this ritual, guarding you from all lower energies and clearing away any blocks to your awareness.

2 | Using the flame from the candle, ignite your sacred blend in a heat-safe dish and gently fan the smoke over yourself.

3 | Now place your Amethyst crystal in the palm of your hand, close your eyes and quiet your mind. Amethyst is a very powerful stone that is known to promote spiritual awareness and psychic abilities. Try to turn off all thought and simply tune in to the energy of your crystal.

4 | Now envision that a purple energy is beginning to flow from the crystal to your hands, gradually moving up your arms and through the rest of your body.

5 | When you feel that you have been enveloped in this warm purple energy, it is time to say your affirmation, which comes in the form of a question: 'What would you have me know?'

6 | Clear your mind and simply wait for the answer. Do not try to force thoughts. Simply observe anything – images, sounds, words or feelings – that comes to your awareness.

7 | When you feel the ritual is complete, extinguish your candle and sacred blend, and thank your higher power.

AFFIRMATION
*'What would you have
me know?'*

10 REJUVENATION

Relaxation · Renewal · Serenity

Renew your spirit with this powerful relaxation blend, which has been conveniently combined into a fragrant bath bomb. The invigorating lemongrass and eucalyptus combo is intended to soothe your nerves, release stress and help you to recharge after a long day.

BLEND

- *Bicarbonate of soda, 115 g (4 oz)*
- *Epsom salts, 60 g (2 oz)*
- *Cornflour, 30 g (1 oz)*
- *Citric acid, 60 g (2 oz)*
- *Dried lavender buds, 2 tbsp (optional)*
- *Coconut oil, 3 tsp*
- *Lemongrass essential oil, 1 tsp*
- *Eucalyptus essential oil, 1 tsp*
- *Soap colouring, 1–3 drops*
- *Water, 1 tbsp*
- *Camomile flower*

TOOLS

- *Mixing bowl*
- *Measuring jug*
- *Whisk*
- *Bath bomb mould*
- *Spoon*

Ritual

1 | In a large bowl, whisk together the bicarbonate of soda, Epsom salts, cornflour, citric acid and dried lavender buds (if using).

2 | In a small cup, mix the coconut oil, essential oils, soap colouring and water.

3 | Very slowly add the liquid to the large bowl and whisk quickly. This must be done in small, gradual doses so as not to activate the solution.

4 | Press a camomile flower into the centre of one half of your mould, and fill it with the mixture. Once both halves of the mould are full, press them together and fasten. Allow this to set in the refrigerator for 30 minutes or overnight at room temperature.

5 | When it is ready, use a spoon to gently tap the outside of the mould, before releasing the bath bomb from the plastic.

6 | Add to your bath any time you need to release stress and regroup. While you allow yourself to soak up this fragrant blend, breathe deeply in meditation, while mentally repeating the simple yet powerful affirmation, 'I am that I am', which is intended to help you feel a stronger sense of alignment with your higher self.

GOOD VIBES

Energy Boost · Joy · Positive Outcomes

Turn to this ritual as a quick pick-me-up several times throughout the day, or any time you need it. This vibrant mist is designed to provide an instant energy boost physically and mentally, while inspiring a windfall of luck, love and favourable outcomes.

BLEND
- *Filtered spring water*
- *Grapefruit essential oil, 10 drops*
- *Peppermint essential oil, 10 drops*
- *Rosemary essential oil, 5 drops*
- *Vanilla essential oil, 5 drops*
- *Witch hazel, 1 tbsp*
- *1 mojo wish bean*

CRYSTAL
- *Small Citrine*
- *Small Rose Quartz*

TOOLS
- *60 ml (2 oz) spray bottle*
- *Pestle and mortar*

Ritual

1 | Fill one-third of your spray bottle with filtered spring water. Add all the remaining blend ingredients except the mojo wish bean and shake well.

2 | Using a pestle and mortar, crush the mojo wish bean. As you do so, think of one wish or desire you hold for your life. Sprinkle the dust into the spray bottle, while envisioning this outcome manifesting in your life.

3 | Run your Citrine and Rose Quartz crystals under water to clear them of unwanted energy, while mentally asking that they are cleansed and charged with their original purposes. Drop them into the bottle, close the lid tightly and shake well.

4 | Spray this mist while declaring the affirmation any time you wish to inspire positive energy or elevate your mood.

AFFIRMATION

*'Thank you for the miracles. All in your perfect ways, and
all in your perfect timing.'*

12

SELF LOVE

Self-Esteem · Self-Worth · Personal Empowerment

Designed to assist with easing stress and emotional trauma, this blend is an energetic cleanser that will fill your space with a warm aroma. Allow the Self-Love Ritual to envelope you in its comforting energy, while helping to stabilise emotions and promote an overall sense of strength, self-worth and personal empowerment.

BLEND
- *Palo santo*
- *Rose*
- *Thyme*
- *Cinnamon*

CRYSTAL
- *Rose Quartz*

TOOLS
- *Twine*
- *Mirror*
- *Heat-safe dish*
- *Feather wand*
- *Apple*

Ritual

1| Standing in front of a mirror (preferably one that is full length), light your sacred stick in a heat-safe dish, gently fanning the smoke over your mirror image. Ask your higher power to bless this ritual with love.

2 | While holding the apple in one hand and the Rose Quartz against your heart, gaze into the reflection of your own eyes.

3 | Repeat the words, 'I nourish you with love. Thank you, I accept this love.' This is a very powerful technique that is designed to sink deep into your subconscious mind. Say these words as many times as it takes to feel a distinct shift in your heart.

4 | When you feel this sense of completion, eat the apple as a symbol of the nourishment of love that you have given to yourself.

5 | Thank your higher power, asking that this sense of self-love remain with you always. You may choose to carry your Rose Quartz with you daily in your purse or pocket as a reminder of the unconditional love you have accepted from yourself.

AFFIRMATION

'I nourish you with love. Thank you, I accept this love.'

13 FEMALE EMPOWERMENT

Intuition · Balance · Emotional Strength & Stability

One of the greatest gifts of womanhood is our innate ability to connect on a deep level with our emotions, a skill that allows us to offer profound levels of intuition, creativity and empathy. Turn to this ritual, which is designed to awaken the strength of your divine feminine, should you find yourself in need of channelling these great gifts — such as if you work in a male-dominated office, or after a relationship breakup — to inspire confidence and inner strength.

BLEND
- *Sweetgrass*
- *Rose*
- *Lotus*
- *Queen of the meadow*

TOOLS
- *Twine*
- *Heat-safe dish*
- *Feather wand*

Ritual

1 | Step outside, preferably barefoot, and find a comfortable, quiet place to sit.

2 | Ask your higher power to bless this ritual, connecting you with the energy of the divine feminine.

3 | Light your blend and gently fan the smoke over your body. As you do this, close your eyes and feel your legs and hands sink deeply into the grass and the earth beneath you.

4 | Now imagine that slowly your body is beginning to sprout roots. These roots continue to grow, sprawling further into the ground with each exhalation. Imagine this for a few minutes until the sense of rootedness becomes so firm that you suddenly have the feeling of being entirely unshakeable. See, in your mind's eye, that these imaginary roots that you have sprouted are now drinking in the vitamins and water from the soil, taking in every ounce of nourishment that Mother Earth has to offer.

5 | Now sit for a few minutes, silently repeating the affirmation until you feel a renewed sense of strength within you.

6 | When you have finished, extinguish your sacred stick and make a small hole in the soil to bury your blend. Thank your higher power to close this ritual.

AFFIRMATION
'For all that is birthed and all that is
bloomed, this strength is
owned within me.'

14 CORD CUTTING

Releasing Pain · Making Progress · Stepping Forwards

There are times in life when we must cut the ties of our past in order to fully move into the life that is intended for us. This ritual is designed to assist in releasing old and unwanted habits, patterns, relationships and traumas. Using the power of gratitude to address the past, present and future, turn to the Cord-Cutting Ritual after a breakup or the loss of a job, or to release emotional wounds of any kind.

BLEND
- *White sage*
- *Sweetgrass*
- *Handpicked wild flowers*

TOOLS
- *Twine*
- *Three pieces of paper*
- *A pen*
- *Heat-safe dish*
- *Feather wand*
- *Scissors*

NOTE: The remaining blend can be burned as you undertake the creation of a dream board with images representing the new life you wish to attract. You may decide to do this immediately following your Cord-Cutting Ritual.

Ritual

1 | Wrap three small sacred bundles of white sage, sweetgrass and wild flowers. The white sage is intended to assist in the releasing of old thought patterns, while the sweetgrass will replace it with positive energy. Your handpicked wild flowers are a powerful symbol of freedom and grace. With the ability to withstand severe droughts and plant themselves nearly anywhere, allow these flowers to inspire courage and resilience as you cut ties with your past.

2 | On three separate pieces of paper – one for your past, one for your present, and one for your future – write down one thing you wish to release and one thing for which you are grateful.

3 | Using a thin piece of rope or twine, tie each note to a sacred bundle.

4 | In a heat-safe dish, light your first stick (the one that represents your past). Take a few deep breaths and gently fan the smoke over yourself. Ask your higher power to help you to cut ties with the pain of your past.

5 | When you are ready, cut the cord that is holding the note in place. Say the affirmation out loud and then burn the note in your heat-safe dish. Repeat this step with the other two sacred sticks and notes.

6 | When you have finished lighting all three sticks, you may extinguish them for later use. Thank your higher power to conclude the ritual.

AFFIRMATION

'I bless you now and release you from my life.'

15 CALLING ALL ANGELS

Divine Communication · Angelic Support · Protection

At any given moment, there is an invisible force eager to leap into immediate action in order to assist us – all we must do is ask! This simple ritual is designed to call forth an army of angels to provide help with any situation you face, big or small. Use the Calling All Angels Ritual when you wish to receive protection, assistance or divine insights from your angels.

BLEND
- *Angelica*
- *Thyme*
- *Baby's breath*
- *Pine*
- *Clover (optional)*

CRYSTAL
- *Angelite cluster*

TOOLS
- *Twine*
- *Heat-safe dish*
- *Feather wand*
- *White ribbon (optional)*

Ritual

1 | Sit quietly alone and away from distractions. Close your eyes and ask your higher power to bless and protect you as you conduct this ritual.

2 | Light your sacred stick in a heat-safe dish.

3 | Holding your Angelite cluster, close your eyes and take several deep breaths, imagining that a white light is beginning to pour out from the crystal, gradually filling the entire room. As you continue to breathe deeply, look into this light and notice the emergence of several angelic figures. Some are small and fairy-like, and some are so large that they look like they could lead an entire army of angels.

4 | Take your time in becoming aware of their heavenly presence and, when you are ready, state the following prayer: 'Angels I call upon you now. Please provide your divine assistance in this situation, removing all obstacles and transmuting darkness to light. I rest now in your light and love. Thank you for your presence always. And so it is.'

5 | Keep your crystal close as a reminder that the angels are always with you, repeating the affirmation any time you feel the need for support.

16

DIVINE HEALTH

Energy Boost · Vitality · Physical Healing

Inspire good health with this simple ritual in the form of a fresh and aromatic bath bouquet. This invigorating blend will last for weeks in your shower, creating a powerful morning ritual that can be practised daily. Turn to the Divine Health Ritual when you wish to heal a specific ailment, or simply to inspire an overall sense of wellbeing to start your day.

BLEND
- *Eucalyptus*
- *Peppermint essential oil, 10 drops*
- *Lemongrass essential oil, 10 drops*
- *Basil (optional)*

TOOLS
- *Twine*
- *Shower*
- *Sponge*
- *Soap*

Ritual

1 | Gather your eucalyptus and add your essential oils to its leaves. The porous leaves of the eucalyptus plant will soak up the oils and emit their aromas for several days. Tie a tight knot at the base, leaving 15–20 cm (6–8 inches) of string. Hang your bath bouquet on your showerhead.

2 | As you step into the shower, close your eyes and ask your higher power to wash away all lower energies, and replace them with love.

3 | Now step just outside the stream of water and, using your sponge, lather your body with soap. When you are completely covered from head to toe, step back under the water. As you do this, close your eyes and envision the soapsuds as a thick, brown mud. As they rinse off under the water, envision that this brown colour is being washed away.

4 | When the soap is gone, stand underneath the water, feeling the heat of the water at the top of your head. Imagine this heat is a bright, white light that moves through the top of your head and down your neck and spine, flooding your entire body.

5 | When you feel that you are completely recharged by this white light, you may thank your higher power and continue with your shower. Repeat this step daily for 2–3 weeks, or until your bouquet loses its fragrance.

AFFIRMATION

'I immerse myself in perfect divine health.'

17 SWEET SUCCESS

Career Progress · Goal Attainment · Prosperity

This warm and fragrant blend is designed to both stimulate and ground your senses, inspiring dedication, focus and drive. Turn to this ritual when you wish to achieve a new goal, or simply to continue on the path to success, filling your workspace with the aroma of sweet success.

BLEND
- *Orange essential oil, 2–3 drops*
- *Cinnamon*
- *Pine*
- *Daisy pom*
- *Clover (optional)*

CRYSTAL
- *Pyrite cluster*

TOOLS
- *Twine*
- *Heat-safe dish*
- *Feather wand*

Ritual

1 | Go to your workspace at a quiet time, when you won't be disturbed, preferably early in the morning before you start your tasks for the day. Add a few drops of orange essential oil to the cinnamon sticks and ignite your sacred stick. Place it alongside your Pyrite cluster, in a heat-safe dish.

2 | Begin by standing in front of one wall. Close your eyes and ask your higher power to bless and protect this ritual.

3 | Open your eyes and gently fan the smoke in the direction of the first wall using your feather wand. Say the affirmation out loud, while imagining that the wall turns to solid gold.

4 | Turn to the next wall and repeat step 3. Continue until all four walls have been covered in gold in your mind's eye.

5 | When you have finished, remove the Pyrite cluster from the dish and place it on your desk. Pyrite is an incredibly positive energy stone that is known to inspire success in all areas of life. When placed on a desk, it is believed to infuse the workspace with positive energy.

6 | Say the affirmation one last time, before thanking your guides for your ongoing success and prosperity.

AFFIRMATION

'*My actions lead to victory. I am successful at every turn.*'

18 PROTECTION

Physical Safety · Security · Dispel Negative Energy

At any given moment, we have access to a powerful force field of protection by envisioning 'the golden circle', a barrier of white light that dispels negativity and allows only love to enter into our energetic space. The Protection Ritual is designed to help us to call upon this powerful shield, keeping us safely guarded from negative energy and misfortune.

BLEND
- *Pepper*
- *Eucalyptus*
- *Cinnamon*
- *Lavender*
- *Cactus*
- *Basil (optional)*

TOOLS
- *Obsidian arrowhead*
- *Peacock feather*
- *Clear glass ornament*
- *Pestle and mortar*
- *Charcoal*
- *Charcoal burner*

Ritual

1 | Carefully decorate your clear glass ornament with your plants, obsidian arrowhead and peacock feather, creating a protection globe that is representative of 'the golden circle'.

2 | Using a pestle and mortar, grind the remaining herbal ingredients to a fine powder.

3 | Sit in a quiet place where you won't be disturbed and light your charcoal in a charcoal burner. When your charcoal is ready, sprinkle the herbs onto the centre where they will burn.

4 | Now, holding your protection globe in both hands, close your eyes and imagine yourself being surrounded by a protective sphere of love and light. Imagine that this sphere surrounds you and your living space, which from the outside forms the appearance of a giant mirror, reflecting all negative energy outwards and away from you.

5 | When you feel that you have a clear vision of this beautiful golden orb, open your eyes and state the affirmation.

6 | Conclude this ritual by thanking your higher power and hanging your protection globe in a window.

AFFIRMATION

*'I encircle myself with the divine white light of love and protection
and allow only positive energy to affect me.'*

19 NEWBORN WISH

Birth of a Baby · New Mum

The birth of a baby is one of the most miraculous events of life, calling for a truly meaningful ritual to mark the occasion. As newborns are sensitive to smell and smoke, this blend has been combined into a gift jar, containing a special message to be opened on the child's 18th birthday and making a meaningful keepsake that is sure to be treasured.

BLEND
- *Pine cones*
- *Life everlasting*
- *Birch bark*
- *Star anise*
- *Acorns*
- *Lemon peel*
- *Bay leaves*

TOOLS
- *Glass jar*
- *Paper*
- *A pen*
- *Ribbon, lace or jute*

Ritual

1 | Place your ingredients in a jar, making sure that they are fully dried. If you wish, you may add essential oils of your choosing.

2 | On a small piece of paper, write one wish for the child's life. When you have finished, roll it into a small scroll and tie with a piece of twine or ribbon. Tuck it into the potpourri mixture and seal the jar.

3 | Your jar can be decorated with materials such as ribbon, lace or jute. You may also wish to add a tag to include your name, the name of the child and a description of the jar's meaning.

4 | Offer this gift to the child's parents as a meaningful keepsake.

MESSAGE

'A wish is a desire with a destiny.
Open this wish jar on your 18th birthday to uncover my wish for you.'

NEW JOURNEYS

Travel · Life Milestones · New Adventures

This cheerful pineapple and peppermint blend is perfect for those who travel frequently, as it assists in maintaining a sense of wellbeing and rootedness as you come and go from home. Perform this ritual as a welcome home or going away ceremony for a loved one, or as a celebration of a new journey such as a marriage, retirement or graduation. This can also be a powerful ritual if you wish to attract more travel into your life.

BLEND
- *Pineapple leaves*
- *Wild flowers*
- *Peppermint*

CRYSTAL
- *Aquamarine*

TOOLS
- *Twine*
- *Heat-safe dish*
- *Feather wand*

Ritual

1 | Either alone, or with a loved one, find a quiet place outside on the grass and light your sacred stick.

2 | Aquamarine is a calming stone that is often used to inspire safe travels. In ancient times, this gem was kept and carried by sailors for courage and protection as they journeyed out to sea. Hold your Aquamarine to your heart and ask that your higher power bless and protect you in your travels.

3 | Now, using your feather wand, gently fan the smoke towards your body, starting at the very top of your head and slowly moving towards your feet.

4 | When the smoke reaches the soil, state the affirmation out loud.

5 | Extinguish the stick and wait until it is completely cooled. End the ritual by thanking your higher power and burying your sacred stick in the soil, as a symbol of your connection to home.

AFFIRMATION

'I am safely rooted in the soil from which I roam.'

21 ANXIETY

Releasing Stress · Relieving Worry · Alleviating Depression

With a soothing blend of essential oils, this ritual has been designed to reduce stress, anxiety and depression. Perform this ritual quickly and discreetly in your car before heading into work, or as you take a moment to regroup at your desk. It is also known to help with headaches and muscle tension.

BLEND
- *Filtered spring water*
- *Peppermint essential oil, 10 drops*
- *Lavender essential oil, 10 drops*
- *Eucalyptus essential oil, 5 drops*
- *Witch hazel, 2 tbsp*

CRYSTAL
- *Small Kyanite or Sodalite*

TOOLS
- *60 ml (2 oz) spray bottle*

Ritual

1 | Fill one-third of your spray bottle with filtered spring water. Add the remaining blend ingredients. Cleanse your Kyanite or Sodalite crystal by running it under water and then drop it into the bottle.

2 | Spray your mist in the air in front of you.

3 | Take a deep breath, inhaling through your nose for a count of four.

4 | Hold your breath for a count of seven.

5 | Exhale through your mouth for a count of eight.

6 | Repeat this cycle three more times.

7 | Mentally state your affirmation.

22

BIRTHDAY WISHES

Birthday Celebration · Milestone Birthday · New Baby

Like the smooth icing on a birthday cake, this ritual is designed to infuse your special day with the sweetest of energy. Using an irresistible blend that includes notes of vanilla and cinnamon, this ritual will inspire luck, love and positive energy throughout your year.

BLEND
- *Palo santo*
- *Vanilla pod*
- *Cinnamon*
- *Birthday boy or girl's favourite flowers*

TOOLS
- *Twine*
- *3 birthday candles*
- *Birthday cake*
- *Feather wand*
- *Heat-safe dish*

Ritual

1 | Perform this ritual on a loved one who is celebrating a birthday. Light three birthday candles and place them on top of a birthday cake. Then, using the flame from the candles, light your sacred stick and ask that your higher power bless this ritual.

2 | Ask your guest of honour to close their eyes and make three wishes for the upcoming year – one for the mind, one for the body and one for the spirit. As they are doing so, gently fan the smoke over them from head to toe.

3 | When your loved one is ready, he or she may open their eyes and blow out the three special candles.

4 | You may keep the stick burning in the heat-safe dish as the birthday celebration continues.

5 | Thank your higher power and enjoy the cake!

23 FORGIVENESS

Releasing Old Wounds · Overcoming Heartache · Letting Go

Forgiveness is an essential part of healing that must occur if we wish to live our lives to the fullest. This fragrant blend was designed to assist in releasing old wounds and transmuting anger into love and understanding.

BLEND
- *Pine cones*
- *Juniper*
- *Rosemary*
- *Bay leaves*

TOOLS
- *Fire pit*
- *Pen and paper*
- *Newspaper*
- *Twine*

Ritual

1 | Go to an outdoor fire pit on a calm day and build a small fire.

2 | Take a few deep breaths and quiet your mind, focusing on the issue that has been troubling you. The first step in forgiveness is honouring the truth of where we are. With this in mind, write down why you are upset, under a heading that says, 'What is hurting me?'

3 | When you have finished, take a moment to consider all the ways that your anger and pain have served you. Has it allowed you to deflect your guilt by pointing blame? Has it kept you from taking actions that scare you? Has it made you stronger? Our subconscious minds are very effective in only holding on to that which serves us in some way. Take a moment to acknowledge how your lingering feelings of resentment have been serving you, under the heading, 'How has this pain served me?'

4 | Once you have acknowledged where you are and why you have chosen to stay there, the next step is to try to find feelings of empathy. If this is an exercise in self-forgiveness, try to find a way to empathise with yourself. If it is someone else whom you wish to forgive, take a moment to step into his or her shoes and imagine their pain. How has the other person also been hurt in this situation? Write it down under the heading, 'How have they been hurt?'

5 | Finally, ask 'What do I want this pain to become?' Only we have the power to change direction and release that which has been holding us back. Decide right here and now what you wish your anger and resentment to transform into and write it down.

6 | When you have finished, wrap this paper around your sacred stick and add another layer of newspaper, fastening it with a piece of twine. Toss it into the fire. As you watch it disintegrate in the flames, state the affirmation aloud.

'I fully and freely forgive you now.
I bless you and release you from my life.'

24

FRIENDSHIP

Connection · Harmony · Community

Surprisingly, one of the most effective predictors of longevity isn't our physical health — it's our level of fellowship and community, making it so important to inspire positive connections with the people in our lives. Turn to this ritual to deepen existing friendships and attract new ones into your life.

BLEND
- *Chrysanthemum or Dandelion*
- *Rose*
- *Wildflowers of any kind*
- *Queen of the meadow*
- *White sage*

CRYSTAL
- *2 Clear Quartz*

TOOLS
- *Twine*
- *Kraft paper*
- *Note card*
- *Heat-safe dish*

Ritual

1 | Wrap two sacred bundles and tie them tightly, as a symbol of the love that bonds two friends together.

2 | Cleanse your Clear Quartz crystals under running water and ask your higher power that they be cleared of all lower energies. Clear Quartz is known to take on the energies of their owners, meaning that they can be programmed with any wish or intention. Holding one of the Clear Quartz crystals, close your eyes and mentally state the affirmation. When you have finished, fasten it to the base of the sacred bundle.

3 | Wrap both bundles in kraft paper, labelling one with your name and the other with the name of your friend. On a small note card, write down the affirmation and tuck it into his or her bundle.

4 | Gift both bundles to your friend, asking him or her to also state the affirmation on the other Clear Quartz (the one that you did not program) and return it to you.

5 | Burn your sacred bundles at any time, when you are together or apart.

AFFIRMATION

'Through this friendship we are strengthened, blessed and prosper.'

25 AURA CLEANSING

Realignment · Energy Clearing · Chakra Balancing

This ritual, which uses the power of colour therapy, has been designed to recalibrate your aura from head to toe. Turn to the Aura-Cleansing Ritual when you feel that your chakras are out of alignment or add it to your practice to maintain a healthy energetic balance.

BLEND
- *White sage*
- *Myrrh essential oil, 4–6 drops*
- *Nutmeg powder*
- *Your choice of flowers in chakra colours: red, orange, yellow, green, blue, indigo and violet*

TOOLS
- *Twine*
- *Heat-safe dish*
- *Feather wand*

Ritual

1 | Wrap your sacred stick, adding a few drops of myrrh essential oil. Sprinkle on a small amount of nutmeg. Then, using the flowers you've gathered in the corresponding chakra colours, carefully wrap your blend with petals in the following sequence, starting at the base of your wand: red (root chakra), orange (sacral chakra), yellow (solar plexus), green (heart chakra), blue (throat chakra), indigo (third eye chakra) and violet (crown chakra).

2 | Light your sacred stick and leave it to burn in a heat-safe dish. Sit or lie down and close your eyes, asking your higher power to bless and protect your energy while you conduct this ritual.

3 | Take a few deep breaths and imagine that you are at the base of a very tall staircase that ascends into the sky. As you begin to climb this staircase, you notice that the air all around you is red. Breathe in this red until you feel that it has completely flooded your energetic body. When you have finished, you say the affirmation: 'I am a divine being of light. I restore myself to complete energetic alignment.'

4 | Continue to climb this staircase, moving through the coloors in the order they have been placed on your sacred stick, until you reach the very top of the staircase.

5 | When you have finished, thank your higher power for the transformation and ask that your energy be protected throughout the rest of the day.

'I am a divine being of light. I restore myself to complete energetic alignment.'

CROSSING OVER

Celebration of Life • Healing Grief • After-Life Transition

This ritual has been designed to assist in the transition of our cherished loved ones, helping us to see death as a passage and not as an ending. Turn to this ritual to find peace and closure in the event of a passing, or to assist in the transition to the afterlife of a spirit that you sense is lingering in the home.

BLEND
- *Juniper*
- *Birch bark*
- *Wild flowers*

TOOLS
- *Twine*
- *Heat-safe dish*
- *Feather wand*

Ritual

1 | The earth has been connected to the afterlife for thousands of years, as many cultures built tombs and made carvings in honour of loved ones who had passed. Begin this ritual by gathering as much of your blend as possible yourself, with the intention of connecting to Mother Earth, an important part of this blessing. Juniper, birch bark and wild flowers are easily found, so venture outside and explore.

2 | Wrap your blend and find a quiet place to sit, preferably outdoors. Light your sacred stick and gently fan the smoke over your body, asking that your higher power bless and assist in this ritual. Set it to burn in a safe place.

3 | Close your eyes and imagine that you are descending into a dark cave. Breathe deeply as you see yourself moving down further until you reach the very bottom.

4 | As you feel your feet plant firmly on the ground, you see a white light begin to shine in the distance. You look into this light and it shines more brightly with each breath you take, until soon it is completely overpowering. Out of this light, you see a figure emerge. It is the person who has passed. You step towards this person and look into his or her eyes, seeing a deep sense of love and peace in his or her essence.

5 | Now is the time to say anything and everything you wish to say to the spirit who is crossing over. Don't hold back. All feelings are welcome and okay, whether they are positive or negative. Take as much time as you need.

6 | When you have finished, envision that this person is moving back into the light. Once they have gone, state the affirmation and thank your higher power.

AFFIRMATION

'Our hearts are healed and whole as you move into the light.'

27 CREATIVITY

New Ideas · Fresh Perspective · Innovation

This fresh and invigorating blend is designed to awaken your senses, heighten your intuition and get your creative juices flowing. It is an especially effective practice for writers, entrepreneurs and artists. Turn to the Creativity Ritual when you wish to inspire new insights and ideas, or for an extra creative push when completing an important project.

BLEND
- *Rosemary*
- *Orange peel*
- *Cinnamon*
- *Carthamus*
- *Alstroemeria*

TOOLS
- *Twine*
- *Heat-safe dish*
- *Feather wand*
- *Notebook and pen*

Ritual

1 | This simple ritual is intended to be practised first thing in the morning upon waking. Sit or lie in a quiet place where you won't be disturbed and light your sacred stick, taking several deep breaths and allowing the soothing aroma to surround you. Ask your higher power to bless this ritual.

2 | When you are ready, pose the following question to your higher power: 'What miracles would you have me create today?'

3 | Sit in stillness, with the intention of simply allowing the answers to come forth. Take note of any thoughts or ideas that come to mind by writing them down, resisting the urge to filter or interpret. If you feel that your mind is being pulled in another direction, simply re-centre yourself by repeating the question.

4 | Practise this ritual for as long as it feels right. You will know when you have finished. Thank your higher power for the creative insights.

5 | Carry your notebook with you throughout the day, writing down any other ideas that come to mind. This question will work as a powerful creativity affirmation throughout the day, so repeat it as often as you wish.

AFFIRMATION

'What miracles would you have me create today?'

28 OVERCOMING ADDICTIONS

Breaking Habits · Recovery · Lifestyle Improvements

With the stress that can so often accompany our daily lives, it is not uncommon to seek unhealthy escape in things like phones, television, food, drugs or alcohol. This fresh and rejuvenating blend is intended to assist in the releasing of unwanted habits, patterns and addictions, helping you to instead establish a lifestyle of positive and empowering choices.

BLEND
- *Eucalyptus*
- *Pine*
- *Lemongrass*
- *Lemon peel*

CRYSTAL
- *Amethyst*
- *Clear Quartz (optional)*

TOOLS
- *Twine*
- *Feather wand*
- *Water jug*
- *Water*
- *Drinking glass*

NOTE: *This ritual should be used in addition to formal treatment programmes for addiction to drugs and alcohol.*

Ritual

1 | In a quiet place where you won't be disturbed, light your stick and gently fan the smoke over yourself. As the smoke drifts over you, ask your higher power to bless and protect this ritual, while helping to cut all energetic ties with the habit you wish to break.

2 | Close your eyes and breathe deeply, imagining a thick black smog coming out of your lungs as you exhale. This black smog symbolises the lower energies that you have been holding on to in the form of your addiction or bad habit.

3 | When you feel as though all the smog has left your body, open a window to allow this energy to escape.

4 | Fill your jug with water and add a piece of Amethyst. Known as the master healer, Amethyst has been used for thousands of years to help in overcoming addictions. It is known to ease stress, distill our thought processes and help us to make responsible choices. You may also include a Clear Quartz crystal to amplify the Amethyst's energy.

5 | Wrapping your hands around the base of the container, close your eyes and imagine a healing white light moving through your hands and into the jug. This light is a symbol of the positive and empowering choices you will now nourish yourself with.

6 | When you feel as though the jug is overflowing with this positive energy, open your eyes and pour yourself a glass. Drink the water while mentally stating the affirmation and thanking your higher power. Drink one glass daily until the water is gone.

29 AFTER AN ARGUMENT

Forgiveness · Understanding · Letting Go

We've all been in the unfortunate position of sitting in a room and collecting ourselves after an argument has taken place. The air feels thick and hot, and all we want to do is to feel a sense of restored peace. This blend is designed to clear a room of lower energies and help us to heal and reset after an argument has occurred.

BLEND
- *White sage*
- *Lavender*
- *Pink roses*
- *Dried white yarrow*

CRYSTAL
- *Rose Quartz*

TOOLS
- *Twine*
- *Heat-safe dish*
- *Feather wand*

Ritual

1 | Sit quietly in the room where the argument occurred. Light your blend and set it aside in a heat-safe dish.

2 | Holding your Rose Quartz, the stone of compassion and unconditional love, close your eyes and ask your higher power to heal your heart. Ask for mutual understanding and restored peace with regards to the situation.

3 | When you have finished, place the stone at the entrance of the room, preferably in a hidden spot, as a symbol that only love should enter the room from this point forwards.

4 | Open a window or door to allow negative energy to escape.

5 | Now, taking your sacred stick and feather wand, direct the smoke into all four corners of the room, while repeating the affirmation at every wall.

6 | Close the ritual by thanking your higher power for the complete healing that has occurred.

AFFIRMATION
'I release all wounds and restore us to the light.'

30 BLESSED MARRIAGE

Engagement · Marriage · Anniversary

If you or someone you know is getting married or celebrating an anniversary, this ritual offers a unique way to add meaning to the event. Add this ritual to your special day, or perform it quietly alongside a few close friends and family members. Not only does this blend make a powerful cleansing recipe, it also looks stunning as a bouquet for the bride or wedding party. Combine leftover lavender buds and rose petals to make a lovely biodegradable wedding toss.

BLEND
- *Lavender*
- *Globe thistle*
- *Pussy willow*
- *Lagurus (also known as 'bunny's tails')*
- *Queen of the meadow*
- *White roses*

TOOLS
- *Twine*
- *Ribbon or lace (optional)*
- *Heat-safe dish*
- *Feather wand*

Ritual

1 | Designed to be incorporated into a wedding ceremony, engagement or anniversary party, burn this blend in a heat-safe dish alongside a group of loved ones.

2 | The bride and groom should assign a leader to direct the ritual, as well as a handful of family members and friends to participate. One by one, ask that each person approach the bride and groom, stating the affirmation aloud and gently fanning the smoke towards the couple.

3 | When everyone has done their part, the entire group is asked to state this affirmation aloud together.

4 | The leader of the ritual should say a quick prayer of gratitude to conclude the blessing.

AFFIRMATION

'From this union we are blessed.'

INDEX

A

abalone shell 14
addictions ritual 120-121
After an Argument 122-123
air, fresh 56, 78, 122
All Purpose 76-77
Amethyst 25, 72, 76, 82, 120
angel ritual 94-95
Angelite 94
Anxiety 106-107
apple 28, 88
Aquamarine 104
argument ritual 122-123
aromatherapy 20
Aura Cleansing 114-115

B

basil 31
bath bomb 84-85
Birthday Wishes 108-109
blending 50-51
Blessed Marriage 124-125
bowls, sacred 19
burner, charcoal 14, 100
burning, blend 54-55

C

Calling All Angels 94-95
camomile 29
candles 68, 108
Carnelian crystal 80
case studies 9
chakra colours 114
charcoal 14, 19, 100
cinnamon 35, 98
Citrine 25, 66, 78, 86
citrus plants, blending 51

cleaning home 56, 78
Clear Quartz 25, 68, 112, 120
clover 32
Confidence 80-81
Cord Cutting 92-93
Creativity 118-119
Crossing Over 116-117
crystals, sacred cleansing with 24-25
custom ritual 62-63

D

dill 37
Divine Health 96-97
dream ritual 72-73

E

empowerment ritual 90-91
energy, protecting your 58
essential oils 20
eucalyptus 38, 96

F

feather wand 14
Female Empowerment 90-91
fire pit 110
florals, blending 51
flowers
    camomile 29
    hibiscus 40
    lavender 36
    lotus 30
    rose 43
Forgiveness 110-111
Friendship 112-113
fruits
    apple 28
    lemon 33

G

ginger 39
Golden Touch case study 9
Good Luck 66-67
Good Vibes 86-87

H

health and safety 10
health ritual 96-97
herbs
    basil 31
    dill 37
    peppermint 41
    rosemary 34
    sage 44, 92
    sweetgrass 45, 92
herbs, blending 51
hibiscus 40
Home, Sweet Home 78-79

I

incense 22

J

jar, glass 102
journeys ritual 104-105

K

kit, sacred 14-25
Kyanite 25, 74, 106

L

lavender 36
lemon 33, 70
lotus 30
love rituals 68-69, 88-89
luck ritual 66-67

M

makko powder 22
marriage ritual 124-125
matches 14
meditation 24
morning ritual 70-71
mortar, pestle and 14, 100

N

New Journeys 104-105
Newborn Wish 102-103

O

oils, essential 20
ornament, clear 100
Overcoming Addictions 120-121

P

palo santo 42
peppermint 41
pestle and mortar 14, 100
plants 14
    burning loose 54
    burning wrapped 54
    clover 32
    eucalyptus 38, 96
    ginger 39
    yarrow 47
plants, sacred 28-47
prayer, sacred 61
protection method 58
Protection 100-101
Psychic Wisdom 82-83
Pyrite 25, 66, 98

Q

Quartz
    Clear 25, 68, 112, 120
    Rose 25, 78, 86, 88, 122

R

Rejuvenation 84-85
resins, blending 51
Rise & Shine 70-71
ritual, custom 62-63
Romance 68-69
rose 43
Rose Quartz 25, 78, 86, 88, 122
rosemary 34

S

sacred bowls 19
sacred plants 28-47
sacred prayer 61
sacred spray 20, 72, 80, 86, 106
sacred sticks 16
    criss-crossed 53
    drying 52
    wrapping 53
safety, health and 10, 55
sage 44, 92
sage, white 92
sand, bowl of 55
Selenite 25
Self-Expression 74-75
Self Love 88-89
smoke cleansing, power of 8-9
Sodalite 106
space, preparing your 56
spices
    cinnamon 35
spices, blending 51

spray bottle 14
spray, sacred 20, 72, 80, 86, 106
stagnant energy 22
sticks, sacred 16
    criss-crossed 53
    drying 52
    wrapping 53
Stupid Cupid case study 9
success ritual 98-99
Sweet Dreams 72-73
Sweet Success 98-99
sweetgrass 45, 92

T

tea infusion 70
tree family, blending with plants
    from 51
twine 14, 74
    gold 66

V

vanilla 46

W

wand, feather 14
water, bowl of 55
wood
    palo santo 42
wooden sticks, burning 54

Y

yarrow 47

Rituals are in **bold.**

CREDITS

For Kai, Elliot and Henrik — you are my favourite kind
of inspiration.

In gratitude to Marta Queen — your spiritual guidance and wisdom
has meant so much to me.

BIBLIOGRAPHY

Essential Oils Desk Reference (Essential Science Publishing,
Second Edition, 2000)

*Sacred Herbs: Your Guide to 40 Medicinal Herbs and How to Use Them
for Healing and Well-Being*, Opal Streisand (Sterling Publishing, 2018)

The Secret Language of Flowers, Samantha Gray (CICO Books, 2015)

Sacred Space: Clearing and Enhancing the Energy of Your Home, Denise Linn
(Rider, New Edition, 2005)